Home Thoughts from a Broad

Isabel White

Edited by Claire Webb

Home Thoughts from a Broad first published in May 2014 by
Alarms & Excursions
3rd Floor
4-8 Ludgate Circus
London
EC4M 7LF
(www.alarmsandexcursions.com)

ISBN 978-0-9565761-1-8

Printed on recycled paper by
Print Resources, Hertfordshire, England

Home Thoughts from a Broad

For Patricia

Home Thoughts from a Broad

ACKNOWLEDGMENTS

With due apologies to those who may inadvertently have been omitted, the author gratefully acknowledges the support and encouragement of fellow poets, journal editors, poetry competition judges, friends and colleagues for their support and encouragement in the production of this book. Thanks are due in particular to: Andrew Borge; the Bridewell team; poets and regulars at the Bar des Arts, Guildford; Jules and Sue at Crystal Palace Subway; fellow desvalidas, Cassandra Mathews and Alison Johnson; John Hegley; Jazzman John Clarke; Agnes Meadows and all the Loose Muse writers in London and Manchester; John McKiernan and the Platform-7 team in the UK and the Netherlands; Samantha Bond, Robert Hardy, Michael Horowitz, Maxine Peake and Jo Shapcott for encouraging words; Elvis McGonagall; members of the Poetry Society stanza in Greenwich; Claire Webb for her diligence in editorship and other London poets, too numerous to mention.

Cover photograph courtesy of Amy White. Photograph of the Restaurant de la Réserve in Nice by Jean Gilletta, reproduced by courtesy of The Bibliothèque du Chevalier de Cessole-Nice. Photographs on pages 22 and 27 courtesy of Andrew Moffatt. All other photographs are the work of the author.

ABOUT ISABEL WHITE

Isabel writes both for the page and the stage. She has performed regularly throughout the UK, at Shakespeare and Co in Paris, and in Rotterdam. Her favourite London haunts are The Corset Club, Mr Ed's Mini Matcham and at John Hegley's Elevenses. She has also appeared at a number of Festivals - at Brighton Festival Fringe, Greenwich Jazz Festival, Guernsey International Literary Festival, Keats Festival and Wickham Road Jazz Festival..., and has shared a stage with, amongst others, Kate Fox, Elvis McGonagall, Michael Horowitz, Jo Shapcott and the late Fran Landesman. Isabel also mounts bespoke events such as Desvalidas (music and poetry from Spain) and Ja Burns, a Scots Jamaican mash up Burns Night.

Isabel's work has appeared in more than a dozen journals, including Keats Festival Anthology, Succour, Wordsmyth, Loose Muse, The Sun Also Rises, Trespass, Poetry Pearl... Alongside a variety of essays and non-fiction works, she has had three short stories published, two in the Loose Muse Anthology and another in New Trespass. Her first collection, *Death & Remembrance*, was published in 2010 by Alarms and Excursions.

She also provides creative poetry input to multiple arts company Platform 7. Isabel curated the poetry for the hugely successful Up The Line remembrance event in Brockley in November 2009 and 2010, and Margate 2011, attracting a combined audience of over 1000. Her remembrance poem, co written with American poet Nancy Esposito and UK surrealist Ronnie McGrath, was performed across ten London Underground stations on Remembrance Day 2012. Her work was also performed at Silent Cacophony in 2013. She founded and ran for 3 years the Chichester Stanza of the Poetry Society and is a regular at the South East London stanza.

Isabel was runner up in the 2013 BBC Radio 3 Proms Poetry Competition (judged by Ian MacMillan, Don Paterson & Judith Palmer), and was a prize winner in the Guernsey International Literary Festival 2014.

In 2005, she was poet in residence at First Stop in Darlington, in 2009 for Brendoncare, in 2011 for Platform-7 in Margate and again in Catford in 2013. She is currently working on an installation piece for the Crystal Palace subway. "Isabel White—a woman of more tongues than I'd realised'—Bernadette Reed, *Talking Rhythm.*

...'but the highlight was the poetry of Isabel White: sharp, not coarse; witty, not crowd-pleasing.'—Paul Taylor, *Trombone Poetry.*

CONTENTS

PART ONE: BLIGHTY

PART TWO: THE GRAND TOUR

PART ONE: BLIGHTY

Home Sweet Home

BUS STATIONS I HAVE KNOWN [1]

Bus stations I have known
great and grand, and termini,
not in my mind's eye
but rooted in the land.

Bus stations I have known
small and rare,
and bus stops in byways
with no one sheltering there.

Bus journeys I have missed;
a lover's kiss to air instead of lips
on foreshortened trips
to destinations where

I arrived alone.

Valetta Bus Station, August 1968

JEZREELS, MAGPIE ROAD. ALL THE DOCK ROAD STOPS [II]

Every man jack here,
forty years' on jankers,
eight bells' toil where the navy anchors;
all our days are smithereens.

Now the sun's well past the yardarm,
one more dicky run ashore;
back in number one smithery—
all kit, for Monday, spoon spit shiny.

SHANTY III

It's a gor' blimey, blisterin' hot, crazy cockleshell day,
the world is my oyster in Whitstable bay.
Hop pickers, pop pickers
lolly lickers in winklepickers,
brilliantined crimpers with shrimps and champers,
floosies with picnic hampers,
spill out of stations and charabancs galore,
as the sea chamfers the shore and shingle lingers
between the toes and fingers of tiny tot and stevedore.

Where wherries and ferries ply the coast at Seasalter,
cod loins are caught between the groynes
by hook and by crook.
Bints and blokes
and barnacled old soaks,
the missus and the sprogs with their lazy dogs in tow,
and my seersucker skin and blister,
salamander pink with her diamond geezer,
gather on the foreshore
to watch the show.

Muscle squares up to mussel,
and at sundown
done in and dirty,
the hoi polloi conga back to town.
So much krill consigned to landfill.

SEPTIC ISLE ^{IV}

I

Benet and Marshall's Famous Troubadours,
we sweep down Marine Drive,
trash Montgomeries,
trade cash for eels,
liquor and mash,
gorn deaf, gorn blind, gorn 'ome.

Martyrs to thrombosis,
astride our Bucyrus,
we slingshot,
tilt,
feed the slots,
tongues curled round a sugar priapus,
pink hair of heaven.

II

Suited and booted,
in God fearing flannel,
from the summit of the dunes, he summons us sinners;
delivers his ministry,
sermon on the mountain of fire and miracles.

(Rumour has it, he's a Ugandan prince;
she cleans toilets in Enfield)

PLANET THANET ^v

I miss McGill,
thrills cheap as chips,
waves that slapped and tickled the shore,
where hot boys and fickle girls
kissed me quick.

Days spent cruising the tubs
and hot licks in pubs and clubs
where dockers' sons,
some mods, some rockers,
traded punches over Judy.

Today, it is still copasetic;
no Tears for Fears,
no cavalcade of motley busketeers,
just, beachside, burkababes
in hot kabbadi
with Ikbal (he's the daddy).

That's where I prefer to reside,
keep watch on the pernicious briny,
where the seditious lie toe to toe with the malicious,
where my Mr Boombastick Captain Fantastic,
mixes the vibes for the capricious and the bootylicious.
(How he hip hops in those flip flops)

Now the fast trains are here,
Margate is further away than ever.

PUCKERLIPS NOW[VI]

Dover marine,
in the shadow of the flyover,
where legover follows rollover,
in the curtained cab of the curtainsider,
she comes up for air,
breasting the cab window,
naked as a baby,
legs spread to reveal her harbour,
and receive him as he docks...

Intussen wacht zijne vrouw,
op hem, thuis in Enschede
but he is not coming home today.
He's too busy getting his end away.
He's the Lord Warden of this sink port
(for now anyway).

WOOLF HAIKU ^{VII}

It's a bloody long way
to the lighthouse
and no one ever gets there.

SHORT WAY DOWN ^{VIII}

One step away,
and he's out of this world,
ripped sails unfurled,
over jagged, ragged
rock roosts,
dumbstruck,
too late for regrets...

This has become, for some at least
The Journey of a Lifetime.

It did for him.
It wouldn't do for me.

MIND THE GAP [IX]

Not wanted on voyage,
the coastguard's gaff
does its shabby shilly shally;
its singular terrace,
faffed in less than gay abandon.

Coping stones don't;

the dog's gone.
...

Across the way, in the café;
Sea eats the seats beneath our feet
a yard a year.
But we should be OK for a decade or so
before we're washed away;
unless the sea gets bored
with all that froth and bluster;
not want us to outstay,
tip us unceremonious
into the briny.
So we up sticks.

Birling Gap.
Just a hiatus in nature's saunter.
She's joined the Ramblers,
eyeing up land
ripe for redevelopment.

HI DI HI, SEATON ×

Trains no longer call at Seaton;
disgorge campers for Warners
like they did fifty years ago,
when our itsy bitsy world was
ever so teeny weeny;
in lemon and turquoise bikini,
poolside, prepubescent,
goosed and goosepimpled,
the world in our water wings,
wet dreams in clotted cream.
We were sixteen
back when statistics were vital,
two stunners on the arms of scunners.

Now we sip flagons of Otter
in the Anchor along the bay
where mackerel boats tie,
streams run the high street amidships
down to where, cloaked in sparkle,
cine spools rust beneath rock pools
and we, northern crustaceans,
crab-clawed and back bowed,
harbour regrets in lobster nets.

SKEGGIE XI

Joan Jett
on air guitar in the Tower Casino
conjures on-screen adulation,
from posses of tipsy bandit jockeys,
stop-still downhill racers,
formula one boredom beaters,
while we repair to Donertello.

The Soul Weekender beckons.
Aladdin lurks where you least expect him,
showers you in rare and exotic vinyl
spirited in from far-off lands
(like Birmingham
'Alabams').

ROUGH WEATHER ABROAD [XII]

Puttin' out bruff
from down Sea Palling;
them Norfolk bors,
dab hands at settin' hives,
'til, swaddled in Noah's Arms,
sun kisses moon
on a rafty sea.

Fish trains run all night
for glats a shillin' a pint
off the back of a barrow in the shadow of Bow;
Tubby's punters fair clammed
an' dint care where you found 'em,
as long as there's jelly and vinegar
an' yew hent a pint to wash 'em down;
your sorrows, like the sailors what caught 'em,
fit to drown.

Norfolk Dialect:

Bruff:	*hearty*
Bors:	*boys*
Fair clammed:	*very hungry*
Glat:	*eel*
Hive:	*trap for eels*
Noah's arms:	*cumulus clouds*
Rafty:	*windy, draughty*

BRINE MAIDEN XIII

O Capstan, my capstan!
charismatic Sole Baywatcher,
wind lass with samphire necklace,
prismatic essence of luminescence,
through your hilltop zoetrope,
cast your Cyclops eye
over us,
shy ness of lubbers;
spindrift exiles in a shadowlandscape;
ranged over many a margent mile,
salt sea dancers, Adnams Style.

Southwold Lighthouse

R FRIENDS IN THE NORTH? XIV

South,
you are full of deniers
and I am one.

Why did you lie to me;
seduce me with your balmy notions,
pile up my table with plenty,
wrench me from a land of iron and poetry,
where spades are spades,
and kinfolk,
are always found wanting?

You do not speak for me.

Still, I can't quite shake you off;
route out of my roots.
Another country it may be,
but now, I see it clear,
my country.

I will go back. I'm sure I will.

BELOW PENDLE [xv]

We dipped skinny in the rippling Ribble;
chased the minnows' glint in the shallows,
their silver suits snagged in gossamer nets
purveyed by Frank's emporium[1] .

Careful to keep upstream of cows,
in eddies fit to freeze a mammoth,
we swallowed more than pride;
and on an ebbing tide swept up,
and sometimes downstream
were half drowned,
as witches might be found,
whistling downwind;
who swung from gallows
or fuelled a pyre of faggots,
being goats to scape
a hostile landscape.

[1] *F.W.Woolworth*

BILBERRIES ON PENDLE [XVI]

Two mile up over bluff and beck,
over shanks of scree,
I stump up the hard way,
from the fields round Barley...,

jiggered.

At Apronfull[2] ,
tumbling deep into Ogden Clough,
Spring's cherry red promise,
nests from the north wind's blowsy mazurka,
on untrammelled, peat perfect clod,
no skanky sheep hobbled and braying,
only soaring hawks,
peewits.

Scatter my ashes on these bushes,
blue velvet bandits,
Pendle's peculiar edelweiss,
riding their emerald Kilims,
in purple purdah 'til mid summer,
when the reaper comes combing.

[2] *53°51'N, 2° 19' W: Bartholomew's Half Inch Series, Great Britain Sheet 31*

THE WHITE HOUSE ACROSS THE BAY [XVII]
(Midland Hotel, Morecambe)

Effortlessly chivalrous,
devoted to Eric Gill
and serious pursuit of my pleasure,
Gerald parks the Siddeley.

We cocktail, dash, sunshade,
parade before Ravilious' delirious vines,
and on snow white linen,
taste French fancies,
through teardrops of Earl Grey.

Then we migrate;
chase wigeons, teals and dunlins;
take sarnies and umbrage,
from the Prom to Happy Mount Park
and its tableaux of dark delight,
to far fells beyond Bayko bay...

Later, on the Slow and Dirty;
we inhale Green Ayre,
doze on horsehair,
muss Windsors,
fix lips in mirrors,
practise moquette etiquette;
lower straps, 'til we clear Caton,
free Saltaire, flying South.

Midland Hotel Morecambe

LODGING COMPLAINTS XVIII

In the house of doilies and embrocation
the hopes of the nation
rest on tenterhooks;
lovers' furtive looks;
whispered "*Morning*!"
The battleaxe is imminent,
her parlour patter,
licenced to shrill;
as you peck at toast,
a tirade
against the common brigade
who have the temerity.

And we,
athletic of foot and fearing reprisal,
purloin the Coal Tar soap and Izal.

RIVER CAVES XIX

Like them mardy folk from Goosnargh,
We strike out for far-flung places.
In tiny ships we sail the streets
to papier-mache Machupichu,
amid the screech of raffia parakeets.

I have seen chullo and alpaca
on the heads of beggars in Peru,
but for Lanky folk and scousers,
the River Caves
will do.

THE COINCIDENCE OF MY DAD AND AMY JOHNSON IN GLEN HELEN ^{xx}

17th April 1933,
Amy Johnson planted a tree.
17th April 1944,
Fraser crashed,
(as she had done before)
before he planted me.

ARNEMETIA ^{XXI}

Fomenting in her limestone lair,
the Buxton lush whose azure hair
spouts steaming from this frosted well;
romancing Goddess of the Grove
doling out her lixir love
to Romans, and the Stuart Queen,
those who come to see, be seen,
or simply take the air.

She reappears,
to spear with her January ice javelins, Ashwood's cliffs,
a serenade in limpid licks, the winter river riffs,
as they exhale down to Millers Dale.

Wettest of wenches,
she who sought to cure now quenches,
and any day now will evaporate,
only to precipitate
her encore, in millennia.

WITH PAULINE MATTHEWS IN THE ARTS TOWER ^{XXII}

Ride the paternoster with me Kiki.
Oh, let's go up 19 floors into the sky.
There's no need for chillin' at the Bully
with Carmelo, you and I.
No music is sweeter than the notes you sing
with Carmelo you and I.
There's no need for chillin' at the Bully
So, let's go up 19 floors into the sky.
Ride the paternoster with me Kiki.

SONG FOR THE MINERS

(*Finest choir in all the land, Treorci*)

Every pit that ever bore a man out dead
and a widow to weep and children to keep
has shaped this land.
Caps once hung on a pithead peg
now wrung in despair.
Lamps that once lit the black gold
light the way for these listless souls.
It's a long time since a pick was swung in anger here,
God knows no right minded soul would want to,
but the ghosts of many a miner
are still down there,
singing
and swinging.

ON THE OCCASION OF MR. GANDHI'S VISIT
TO THE EAST END [XXIII]

Mahatma,
coatless,
like Stein
without Toklas;
Mohandas,
toughest frail in white percale,
tucked and pinned and bantam binned,
pecking at the brollied throng,
raining on his parade,
all goshes and galoshes.

SHARDENFREUDE XXIV

Avionic adventurers,
half way to paradise,
so near, and yet...

So far so hush!
In cloistered rush to roof on our ascension day,
we exocet[3] to this heavenpier,
aloof to fear of roistering deathdrops.

Unbelievers,
we cleave to a rubic truss,
framing each pretty pixel
of our ribboning encompassed metropolis;
then earthward rebound,
our trajectory -
hundred proof velvet black astral turf.

Fear confounded,
we are easily swayed;
a winning choir
to serenade us,
ear popped, jaw dropped
saints and sinners,
accomplices to leap year
now grounded.

[3] *"Flying Fish", French built anti-ship missile known for its use by the Argentine Air Force during the Falklands war between Britain and Argentina in 1982.*

ROOTS ^{XXV}

Let the record show,
Dad hailed from Hackney;
Mum, your very own Vesta,
your Burlington Bailey,
from Bow.

DAVID BAILEY'S EAST END THANKYOU ^{XXVI}

This is your bailiwick,
where you do your shadow puppet shtick.
Sharp shooter, from Kraydle to grave,
Big noyz for the bombed out boyz
with their barbed wire bouquets,
studied Sunday scowls,
each glitter and grimace
a baby sham of smoggy eyed innocence.

Stripped of gladrags and bones,
She juxta poses, cropped and canned;
Sons and daughters of others come,
see in your aperture
an anonymous chronicler,
still showing, in camera,
but in a knowing way.

PART TWO: THE GRAND TOUR

Hotel La Réserve, Nice

DIRIGIBLE LZ129 [XXVII]

Silently we steal upon the caribou.
One head pops up;
the race is on,
such choreographed panic;
new hunters stalk the afternoon.

But we have no guns,
just cameras.
Some watch through the floor below,
others sip their aperitif;
the pianist in G major, shadowing.

A hundred feet below
frost glistens.
We devour the tundra in hours
in silks and satins.
Tomorrow, we dine above the pyramids.

Between courses,
the Sphinx will kneel in homage
before superior engineering;
Anubis[4] will weep
at our Teutonic hubris.

So, Swift was right,
(my time at Oxford not entirely wasted)
there are cities that ply the skies[5] ,
looking for new lands to conquer,
as the storm clouds gather.

Time to retire to my state room in the sky,
dress for dinner,
draw the chintz
against the birds that might see in,
light a cigarette…

Zeppelin Museum, Friedrichshafen

4 *Greek name for the Egyptian god with the Jackal's head*
5 *Laputa, Gulliver's Travels, Jonathan Swift*

ROTTERDAM SUITE ^{XXVIII}

Aankomst
I aspire
to this low country, this wide sky.

Later, I might ride the absent tide,
mijn oma fiets gently protesting,
straats lang, cool and still,
breeze uninterrupted, lazy and chill.

Sails barely turn in Leiden
as I race by,
disturb a Vermeer moment;
fountains sparkle at de Vink;
I think I might tend my allotment,
till alone
in a shedded shanty town at Voorschoten
'til the sun goes down.

Ornithology
Geen wekker nodig
Rotterdam staat op

In a class of its own;
ship shape and Rotterdam fashion,
every inch paved over
as if to nail the lie of the land
tussen de Maas en de Rijn.

A ding dong humdinger of a city,
all that glisters;
Metallica, spandex, fool's gold.
Rotterdam on the up,
shards of marble
canyons of granite and exfoliate steel.

Cranes roost by the Rabobank
nesting in its black cliffs,
to fashion prosperity
for Rotterdam.

Trams glide harbourside;
kerbs and bollards
delineate the manic manicure
that curbs the upstart cars;
they shimmy and chatter,
clatter over crossings,
in Rotterdam.

I see herrings, glissando, in shellsuit and shades,
shoaling in and out of Vroom and Dreesman
in Rotterdam.

"Stay OK!"
In the home of Holland Amerika,
Nieuw Amsterdam[6]
brimful, chip and pin chipper;
red, yellow, green, all is order,
a permanence of place in an impermanent world.
But the sands still shift, the odd house topples
in Rotterdam.

Erasmus[7]
Did he stride the river in one go?
Did he re-invent the world;
cheat the sea of her birthright?
Does he lie awake at night
wondering if she'll re-claim it?

---

[6] *SS Nieuw Amsterdam, most famous and arguably most luxurious of the Holland
Amerika transatlantic liners, now berthed in retirement in Rotterdam Harbour.*
[7] *Dutch Renaissance humanist*

Hemingway

Literati gather
in shreds and dreds;
ambtenaaren of the spoken word
pressed upon us.
Ondermode on display
Café Hemingway,
en vanavond
Kees en Jeroen, echte dichter
all on Star TV,
Gerrit and Menno (and me)
and, exploding on the night sky,
ING en TNT.

Departure

Op een stille zee, kan iedereen stierman zijn.
Tussen de Maas en de Rijn
dat gaat over land en zand,
maar landen verzanden en zanden verlanden.
Zo gaat het altijd
in Rotterdam.

LIFELINE ^{XXIX}
The figurine is back in the window
so it's safe to come in now
and, if you are already in
it's safe to come out.
No uniforms outside Ten Boom's today.

They came for her yesterday.

Kattensingel, Gouda, Netherlands

AFSLUIT ^{xxx}

Calvinists have no truck with it.
They want to tame the demon.
Arrow straight and narrow,
Een Afsluit, to navigate this dire strait.
Thus do Calvinists divide and rule this spatchcock sea.

Could they subdue the Channel,
or the Atlantic, given half a chance?

Calvinists take root where waves no longer dance;
their women, alone in bruin cafes,
sip coffee,
smoke cigars,

landlocked mermaids.

Afsluit

WILD MENU IN LEEUWARDEN ^{XXXI}

It seemed somehow appropriate,
as I tucked into my dead deer,
I should be serenaded by Mr Cooke.
Pears and wild boar
with vanilla sauce,
starfruit and sprouts.

You send me,
honest you do Sam,
honest you do.

FUNERALS IN BERLIN (BERLIN SUITE) ^{XXXII}
"I am become death, the destroyer of worlds."
Robert Oppenheimer

Denkmal
In ragtime, we recorded
the Weimar intermission,
zwischen Slump und Triumf des Willens.

Spies were everywhere;
silhouetted in doorways,
Isherwood's, Le Carré's;
illumined with torches.

Now, they sweep porches.

So many paper moons, cardboard seas,
canvas skies.

Kristallnacht (Fasanenstrasse)
Then...
egress denied for semites
at the epicentre
of shatter;
of crash and burn.

Now...
entry denied for gentiles,
silence, save for the clatter
of lock, stock and barrel;
preserving pogroms for posterity.

Olympische Stadion Berlin
And where did he sit?
Oh yes,
(where else!)
Aping Nero.

Each Teuton hero,
head held high,
crowned with acorn thorns
presented by some Lorelei.
Their rallying cry we ignored at our peril
and we inherit
(as the meek inevitably do)
the scorched earth.

Subs on the bench,
the Latow brothers showed the way;
for one day at least
the world pretended they were Mensch.

Love Of The Common People (Heinrich Zille)
*"Zille und Ick came in for some schtick
Over drawings of ladies and men
They're in a museum
Where you can go see 'em
Over and over again"*

With an almost total absence of Brille
Zille described Berlin,
in particular the Kasernen
which until then
had not been the concern
of influential men;

his oeuvre,
a far chillier milieu than Schiller,
whether behind the Kamera or as illustrator;
and such uncommon Respekt
from Gerhardt Lamprecht
was shown in his work 'Die Verufenen'.

Picture of Lili[8]
My angel, why so blue?
Who shanghai'd you?
Who plucked those brows?
Which Fraus?

Who tonged those curls?
Who painted those lips?
Who kissed them?
Which girls?

First division
East is east, west is west and the wrong one I have chose.
I reside in the City of Lost Children,
where one in seven is a Johnny Foreigner
and the rest are Huguenots.

Mies En Scène
Those "in the know" commissioned
Van de Rohe,
to fashion from glass, iron and brick
ein Augenblick,
detached
from Realpolitik.
God was in the detail.
(By the Lake Shore
less was always more)

Japs In The Urban Jungle
How many U-boats passed me on the square
hidden in plain sight?
How many more came out last night
to check
that the Nazi and the Stasi really have gone away,
and it's safe once again
to come out to play?

Shapeshifting

From copious cornucopias of Gropius
from Bauhaus to the Rathaus
where now flies the flag
atop a rebuilt Reichstag,
Berlin, ich bin in mein' eigen' Unsinn.

Yes, we too have known sin,
claimed, tamed and renamed it.
We had so little left to show for it
and now you've gone and built all over it.

Konzert Für Zwei Klavierspieler

Major and minor on Bode[9] stoops
a thousand starlings on the roost,
hundert Berliner lulled
beneath a perfekt Berlin backdrop,
hellblau, vermillion evening sky;
soft murmured lyric,
Brahms lullaby,
"Guten Abend, Gute Nacht,
Auf wiedersehn,
Goodbye".

[8] *Marlene Dietrich*
[9] *The Bode Museum*

SO GOOD, THEY NAMED IT TWICE ^{XXXIII}

So schön ist es in Baden Baden
Man muß die Name zweimal sagen

LICHTENSTEIN ^{XXXIV}

Blink, and this Blefescu,
this Grand Fenwick of all the 'stans and 'steins,
where every legit dip on a trip to avarice
flashes his stash;
this Freedonia,
this Rubovia
this Macho Grande,
where every Ron or Reg
hides his wedge,
this Brigadoon,
not departing anytime soon,

is,

just ranks of banks
on clean shaven streets
where, on many an occasion,
avoidance cavorts with evasion.

TEATIME TRAIN TO AROSA

As streets give way to instant gorges,
Big Red,
bumper clipper,
climbs five thousand feet
past pine trees lit by snow,
to find a window
full of scissors.

No clang of Sturm und Drang[10]
here, Switzerland
ding dong bells,
tick tock chimes,
catch a handful of cirrus,
as the choo choo climbs -
its Alpine sonics,
just ice,
still air,
metronomics.

[10] *A late 18th century German literary movement*

SUNRISE OVER THE FISHERMAN'S BASTION ^{XXXV}

This morning, we tripped over shoes of bronze,
brogues, slingbacks and Mary Janes,
petrified, post dive;
all that survived open season
on anyone we didn't like the look of.
We stripped them bare, save for their shoes;
they left them there as a warning.

Bronze shoes abandoned on the banks of the Danube, Budapest

À PROPOS DE NICE? ^{XXXVI}

Where rakes progressed up the beach,
kelp combed in Demy shingle,
parted Pablo and Polo,
Zelda and Fitzgerald,
Moreau and Mann.

Du jour, all was tennis and deep tan,
mais tendre était la nuit
pour les mâitres de l'art de vivre.

They had all seen the light,
becoming interior decorators
with their motionless muse,
fastest of friends,
Picabia's Riviera,
avec Coco, en cocotte;
straight off the Duke's yacht.

Un beau rivage en la Baie des Anges,
mélange des Dada fâcheux,
Lartigue et ses intrigues;
Antipolis,
Santo Sospir,
Lee Miller, nue et inconnue,
Vigo, l'arriviste.

Before Line Renaud had sung a note,
le demi monde a quitté la Côte.

FOR JONI ^{XXXVII}

The voile drapes graze the terrazzo,
henna'd with sand,
here in the palazzo,
afternoon siesta,
of sirocco days, as shadows play
and flowers lay lazy on the piano.

An African wind is calling.
Boats in the harbour are at anchor;
polish and bougainvillea
suggest the scents of summer.

A silk dress dozes on the arm of the chaise
and, shaded from the street below
you, the outsider, incognito,
are the espionage of our encounter.

As the sun rolls over the summit of the day,
sits high and exhales
all the way to the dark, I wonder,
will you sit at the piano,
promise to walk me to the harbour,
where mulattos meander and conversations spark?

The wind is come from Africa,
it carries the dusk through the pink hotel,
wafts in with the aloe vera.
It is so hard to leave her.

HOW TO VIEW VENICE – LESSON ONE ^{XXXVIII}

Like Raffles he steals upon me,
my mahogany playboy;
egregious creature,
he eats me
from fragrant wrist to elbow.

We launch,
buccaneer through the piazza;
from Florian,
survey the horizon for Loren.

Not much time left
before Venice succumbs to indifference.

Venice, once wedded to the sea,
always divorced from reality,
is drowning, not waving,
and is probably not worth saving.

Jetty of the Hotel Danieli, Venice

OSBORNE GODOLPHIN'S NEIGHBOURS ^{XXXIX}
(I gatti della Piramide)

Sshh!
On the Via Caio,
tanti bei canti,
the Keats' cats' scat
out cats the other cats,
out cattin' on kitty littered lawns,
but no dawn chorus,
no caterwaul, forestalls Shelley's shuteye.

Keats' cats
are card carrying catacomb colonisers,
i Custodie Caticani,
tutti capolavori.
sempre in funzione
sempre acattoliche.

Keats' cats have
impeccable combat credentials;
they watch over all the late literati,
Carstens, Corso and Carl Phillippe
as they doze beneath their cypress canopy.

Mystic mogs, mouse trouserers,
Keats' cats, once confronted, swiftly skedaddle.
Sshh!

LEAVING CATANIA XL

We wait on the wall for the slow train
in all its splintered splendour;
windows down,
the mosquitoes' vampiric kisses,
lullaby to sunset,
blow us to Syracuse.

Our steamer, impatient to be underway,
twelve hours to Valetta,
in the moonlight on the quay.

Below decks
i signori in spats and cravats
dine in,
we Sicilian sardines sintered in smuts,
on our rafty palliasse,
lie back and watch the stars.

XLENDI ^{XLI}

You were my Pelagia
The night we bathed naked
in Xlendi Bay.

You were my one idea.
I picture you making lace
on shady days so far, so far away.

Traditional fishing boat, Xlendi Bay, Gozo

SITGES BITCHES

Under parasols in Sitges, Sangria in hand,
the fat and fecund kiss, groom and graze,
pedalos and flying bananas race
beneath a cloudless, cancerous canopy of blue.
We doze beneath our carapace
of factor four, at forty-two,
bringing on a lazy death,
not headlong like lemmings do.

Cheek to cheek
with his speedo date,
oiled up with Piz Buin
the Englishman, a raspberry mivvi[11] ,
wilts,
while metrosexuals promenade,
basting in the searing sun,
and two soggy vanilla cornets in a cocoa butter sea,
from Dewsbury,
sip tea and read "The Lady".

[11] *A popular confection of the 1970s—ice cream with a raspberry flavour iced coating*

MERCAT DE SANT JUSEP
(St Joseph's Market, Barcelona)

Stared out by a dead sheep's head,
skinned and grinning
in the Mercat de Sant Jusep,
I stare back, menace him with oranges
and Tilapia.
I hide in ranks of pomegranates,
throw strawberries, big as breadfruit,
hot, pink and rancid,
while the late trader, the extra virgin,
holas and flirts,
with her ruddy collaborators,
skirts the grass blankets that hide the rats
cats, dogs, medusa,
intestines, rinds and roes
(the market's pluck).
She sluices with buckets of brine,
'til night calls time on the day
and the Mercat is hauled away.

LA SAGRADA FAMILIA XLII
(work in progress)

I wept in the spring sun at love's labour,
the hundred-year span
that began with Gaudi's dream.
Intoxicated
he succumbed to a tram
and died of misinterpretation.

Laid to rest in his wonder well,
the crypt where we now creep
through this choking, dusty hardhat hell,
the lady mason with flame red hair,
serene and patient,
mixes mosaics by day and paella by night.

The sorcerer consumed by his creation,
ponders the imminence of chicken or egg,
settles for both, and sunflowers, and cypresses,
Rodea Japonica and Venus Flytrap,
spiders, snakes and ears of corn.

A salutation in stone,
to violets, palms and passionara,
lotus, acacia, and honeybees…
wave tunnels surfing sand dunes,
starfish, ammonites and flounders
and hand worked boulders in gilt and gold.

Nearer to heaven
I see bleached, skeletal trees,
pumice, limestone, his fossilised promise,
nature's layercake, marble and granite.
Sit here a thousand years
and wait for God's steps to wear away,
see them rise in perpetual spirals, aping Escher.

Now, shielded from sun and rain
in this fractal, helicoidal, hotwired hell on earth
is Gaudi's gaudy masterpiece,
a tower of Babel
brimming with birds and bones,
nests and frogs, the oolitic sentinel
that mocks the monotony
of the City Grid
that shackles it.

I swore I heard,
through cacophonic crashing,
tympanic, jackhammer jabber,
the concatenation of hammer bash and bronze bend,
parakeets, softly calling.

At sunset, Gaudi's ghost inspects
and he hopes they will not finish it
until magma wipes the face of man from this earth,
when, on the eternal Sabbath,
the face of God will shine through,
and He will look like Gaudi.

GRANADA SUITE

Albaicin
(Calle Valenzuela)

I

From his garret,
aperture in the pantiles,
the incidental tourist frames Alhambra.

Through doughnuts of smoke,
with surreptitious cigarette,
he surveys,
from the corner of Horno del Oro
garrulous alleyways.

The caged bird's chatter
shatters with each staccato shock, half heard holas,
of señoras con bragas viejas,
y señoritas in tiny frocks;
and at dawn,
the blare of the gas van's horn
brings calor to every door.

Palm and pine lashed by January rain,
glimpsed as he dives
doorway to doorway,
a hair's breadth splits them,
el trafico,
amurallado.

II

In the Arabian baths
her senses are incensed by frankincense;
and minted caresses

in meagre measures dispensed;
this, her regimen of pleasure principal.
Pummelled to perfection,
undone by lethargy and ghazals[12] ,
she floats to brief oblivion
beneath the steaming stars.

III

He is in a joyous garden
trailing a finger through souks of coriander;
eyeing the coy carp,
he dilly-dallies in lavender green
beneath lemons,
figs and nada.

IV

Perros y gatos run riot in Sacromonte;
trogs with cigarillos menace the stoops;
where the red kite swoops,
clouds hide snowy high sierras,
in the penumbra of the Alhambra.

Alhambra

Ramrod pines,
sentries in scented arbours.
A blush of persimmon, lush cypress,
fern and common blonde[13] ,
rose and sweet pea,
in oceans of evergreen
applaud the geometry of this place;
dissect the math of it.

A cascade through pathways,
labyrinthine,

under variegated ivies
time entwined, to where
fountains spume and spatter;
their gush and guzzle
interrogate this embroidery of wonders,
of bleached birch and blades of acer,
where serrated shade and sparkle
intermingle.

Studded, riveted,
bronzed and bolted,
a conundrum of doors within doors,
veils the odalisques,
intriguing their suitors.

Where once, dynasties were decided,
a weeping prince[14] , wedded to this place
was driven out,
gelded by its beauty.

[12] *Persian love poem*

[13] *Type of orange commonly found in the Mediterranean and North Africa.*

[14] *Boabdil—King Muhammad XII*

JORGE ON MY MIND ^{XLIII}

Jorge is on his burro,
Pesariňha,
(Jorge is on the wagon
these twenty years)
His chimney? Immortalised
in the nation's souvenirs.

Jorge is on his way down the mountain.
The traffic, such as it is,
on the way up.

Nobody cares.

(The Monchique spa remains closed for repairs)

FRAGMENT FROM A WORKMAN'S SIGN IN SILVES CASTLE ^{XLIV}

You will be glad to know, I am sure
that the palace has been recuperated.
They no longer murder the Moors here,
they just murder our language instead.

WHALE WATCHING IN MADEIRA

I

There's a certain swarthe to the locals
head to toe, ecru
(as are all Portuguese).
Surely, they know?

The French are here but few in number;
Germans hold sway,
their collective towel on the lilo of Europe.
But the Brits!

Ah the Brits...
Each Gielgud in shorts,
gently dessicating,
swans around the fountains,
toboggans those cloud-shrugged mountains...

I'm blinded by their trainers—
my hose never quite snowy enough or showy enough
for copper-bottomed colonels,
for these are *hose de loisir,*
über dazzle,
not your everyday apparel for working class Johnnies.

Here, amongst bald pates of expatriates
all is Whicker[15];
scooping all the major prizes
taking the cake and sweet wine
with their jacaranda and frangipani,
upended avocados;
they were born to better things.

As I storm Fortress Reid on my segway
(Formidable as the French might say)

the only guy who always gets his way
is some Jack Daniels;
admittedly, his wallet may be fatter
but the fact of the matter is,
if you are togged up smarter than the swells,
then you're not one.

The Mems, butts of Malmsey,
Meissen faced daughters of empire,
scarce manage a lazy lizard leglift,
cutlass their legs of scrimshaw
with each onset of barbery coarse hair

II

Back at my Hulôt hotel
its all leaks and squeaks,
chambermaid peak-a-boo
and very likely legionnaires;
this shall be my Waterloo.

Still, there are Catholic chimes on a sweet honey Sunday,
bells and blossom,
nocturnal serenade of the oh so chi chi cicadas
ready to pounce.

Hats and chats are de rigeur in this encampment.
Obrigada to our ilha of enchantment.

[15] *Alan Whicker, celebrated travel journalist*

ISIS AND PSORIASIS XLV

Pack my nightshirt, pack my fez.
You can leave the inky biro.
I'm off to find the sauce of the Nile.
I've heard that it's near Cairo.

Waiting in the rain for the steamer,
as we wave goodbye from the jetty,
(Goodbye!)
I'll have my dance round the quayside
With Wilson, Keppel and Betty.

PEELY WALLY TOP RANKIN' ^{XLVI}
(Tempo: Spitter)

Fareweel tae Demerara Kyles o' Bute,
'im fleein' Babylon
gwan for bakra bwoy,
bound for the banks and braes of Montego Bay.
awa' tae gather the creels o' janga,
in scrimpit claes,
in 'im cutty sark,
in the baumy faem.

Nae mair tae dander in the blashie hielands
where the daudin showers
skelp the burns and brackens,
on chitterin' days in this couthie land;
and Bonnie Jean,
winjy dawta, natty dread,
sista sufferer at the Brig o' Doon,
eekin from the dutty eart'
what passin' for a livin'.

II
Word up, whipcracker!
Is there onyone left to hear yer labrish,
dem licious riddims and mixtie maxtie tongues,
blethers soft as a maiden's kiss
in the Gourock gloamin'?

So its fareweel tae the fuff o' the breeze
on yer gizz
the sugh o' the shure,
trinklin linns,
a chillum o' collie...

'Im leavin'
Culloden in the sun.

'Im na gwan raisin' kain from fremit folk;
na jinkin and skankin.
'Im awa' hame tae tax the midges,
balance chill,
seek big tings.

Now 'im breathe easy
as O' Shanter's Covenanter,
leave unanswered
the call of sugar sweet plantation song,
where 'im not grieve the maroons of Monymusk,
Montrose and Mount Stewart;
sept of the Argyll Campbell,
sons of Lochow,
slaves nae mair.

Peely Wally: Glossary

Babylon *Jam.*	The establishment
Bakra *Jam.*	White slave master
Balance chill *Jam.*	Take it easy
Baumy faem *Scot.*	Foamy sea
Big tings *Jam.*	Monetary success
Blashie *Scot.*	Stormy, driving rain
Brae *Scot.*	Hill
Breathe easy *Jam.*	Relax, calm down
Burn *Scot.*	Rivulet
Chillum *Jam.*	Smoking pipe
Chitterin *Scot.*	Shiver
Collie *Jam.*	Marijuana
Couthie *Scot.*	Loving/Lovely
Creel *Scot.*	Basket
Cutty Sark *Scot.*	Short shirt/tunic
Dander *Scot.*	Wander
Daudin *Scot.*	Sideways (of rain)
Dawta *Jam.*	Woman, sister
Dutty *Jam*	Dirty
Fremit folk *Scot.*	Strangers
Fuff *Scot.*	Puff
Gizz *Scot.*	Face
Gloamin *Scot.*	Twilight
Grieve *Scot.*	Over seer
Janga *Jam.*	Shrimps/crayfish
Jinkin *Jam.*	Dodging
Kain *Jam.*	Rent/tax
Kyles *Scot.*	Narrow strait/channel
Labrish *Scot.*	Gossip
Licious *Jam.*	Delicious
Linns *Scot.*	Waterfalls
Lochow *Scot.*	Seat of the Clan Campbell, Scotland
Maroon *Jam.*	Free black warriors
Mixtie maxtie *Scot.*	Confused/confusing

Natty dread *Jam.*	Dreadlocks
Peely wally *Scot.*	Pale (also Jam. Firefly)
Rankin' *Jam.*	Person in charge
Riddims *Jam.*	Rhythms
Scrimpit *Scot.*	Skimpy
Sept *Scot.*	Division/clan descendants
Shure *Scot.*	Shore
Skankin *Jam.*	Dance/skulk/act suspiciously
Skelp *Scot.*	Whip/punish
Sugh *Scot.*	Light breeze, sigh
Trinklin *Scot.*	Trickling
Winjy *Jam.*	Sickly

General Glossary

Jankers: British Forces term for withdrawal or restriction of privileges

Bint (*Arabic*): woman

Copasetic, copacetic (*Fr. Creole*): achievable, lit. something to be coped with

Mardy (*Lancs dialect*): moody, argumentative

Binned: from 'bins' (*cockney slang*)—short for binoculars (i.e. spectacles)

Galoshes: overshoes

Aankomst (*Dutch*): arrival

Omafiets (*Dutch*): bicycle

Ondermode (*Dutch*): underwear

Augenblick (*German*): moment (lit. eye blink)

Fâcheux (*French*): deranged

Mulatto (*pej.*): someone of mixed race

Capolavori (*Italian*): work of art

In funzione (*Italian*): on duty

Acattoliche (*Italian*): dissenter (ing)

Bragas Viejas (*Spanish*): big pants

Amurallado (*Spanish*): walled in

Obrigada (*Portuguese*) (Fem.): thank you

Notes

[I] Almost a sonnet—Ah yes, bus stations, prosaic backdrop to so many brief encounters! I pine for the great bus stations, like Valletta in Malta and, closer to home, Tithebarn Street Preston. As for the rest...

[II] At its height, the Chatham Naval Dockyard employed 10,000 people, most of whom travelled to work by bus from exotically named places like Jezreels and Magpie Road. A friend who was in the Royal Marines in the 1960's showed me how he achieved the gleaming shine on the toecaps of his boots, using heat applied to spoonfuls of polish.

[III] This poem tells the story of London dockworkers on a day out to Whitstable, when that resort was resolutely the province of the labouring classes.

[IV] Benet and Marshall's Famous Troubadours often appeared in Margate, and audiences could repair to Montgomeries to satisfy their craving for jellied eels and pie and mash before or after the performances. Alas, Monty's is no more. This is one of a number of poems that emerged from a residency in Margate in 2011. Septic Isle focuses on fictitious drivers of mechanical diggers manufactured by Ruston Bucyrus, an engineering company established in 1930 and jointly owned by Ruston and Hornsby based in Lincoln, England and Bucyrus-Erie based in Bucyrus, Ohio. Their machines became ubiquitous on building sites all over the UK from that time onwards.

[V] A name synonymous with any seaside holiday in the 1960s, artist Donald McGill whose saucy or obscene (depending on your point of view) postcards filled the post boxes on the seafronts of the nation. It is hard today to see what all the fuss was about, but this did not prevent McGill from being tried for obscenity, and despite original copies of his works selling for thousands today, he made little money from his art. One can't help thinking however that he probably enjoyed it just the same.

Kabbadi is one of many variants of a Sri Lankan game that is very popular with the British Asian community. It is part beach volleyball (without the scant clothing), part tag and part British Bulldog.

[VI] A true story; the author inadvertently stumbled upon a Dutch lorry driver enjoying the distractions of Dover harbour while waiting his turn in the queue for the late ferry. I do not know if he had a wife waiting for him at home, or if he came from Enschede (pronounced 'enskaday'), but it certainly helped with the rhyme scheme! Dover is one of the Cinque Ports, a union of five Kentish towns who collaborated on trade and defence.

VII I really struggled with Virginia's book – it got so tedious. Hence the haiku, it will save you reading it.

VIII I lived for two years below Beachy Head and watched the weekly passage of the coastguard helicopters on their way to recover the remains of another unfortunate soul who had chosen to end their life by jumping from there. It really is a most unpleasant place. In this poem I wondered what it might be like to jump and then have second thoughts on the way down?

IX There had originally been four coastguards' cottages, but when we visited one was already lost to the sea. The café survived as part of a small hotel, but in an increasingly sorry state. You may wish to pay a visit to Birling Gap to see how much remains today (whenever today might be).

X Warner's holiday camp in Seaton, is alas today just a pile of rubble on a brownfield site. It was once the epitome of the seaside holiday camp tradition - regiments of chalets, the poolside beauty parades, knobbly knees contests and canteen food on galvanised trays. In the fifties it was still possible to travel by train to Seaton and there was no need of a car, everything for the holidaymaker being available either in the camp or a short stroll away on the beach. For the seafaring types, mackerel fishing could produce something more exciting and nutritious for the following day's breakfast, though in those days nobody seemed to know what nutritious meant.

Seaton, and its neighbour Beer, are still delightful places to visit and though the camp has gone, the mackerel still cling on to their precarious existence, despite some overfishing.

The polka dot bikini was immortalised in song by Brian Hyland in 1960 (the year of our visit); the song being about a young girl who ill advisedly wore a bikini that was perhaps, with hindsight, a little too immodest, even for a post war teenager. Our memories of that holiday were recorded on spools of 8mm cine film, upmarket precursor to the portable video recorders of decades later (and certainly slightly less tedious than watching uncle Ernie's slide show), although it always took longer to spool the film than show it.

XI Butlin's Skegness is home to many a soul weekender for those like me who are transported by the sounds of soul and original R & B from the 60's and 70's. There is also the wonderful "Tamla Coffee Bar and Record Shop", where I tracked down an American copy of 'Save It, Never Too Late' by Melvin Davis, the last piece of rare vinyl I coveted and had not owned. It cost a small fortune!

XII As you may have gathered by now, I have this fascination with dialect and

accents, Norfolk being one of my favourites. Here it collides with Cockney when the eels arrive at Jewish Tubby Isaacs' stall, to delight the East End locals.
[xiii] One of a number of lighthouse poems, Southwold's reminded me of some Wagnerian Valkyrie who instead of saving lives was luring unsuspecting sailors to their deaths. Obviously I had had too much of that Adnams ale. And who reading this will remember Gangnam Style?

[xiv] The R is a conceit and references the television comedian Peter Kay's spoof of the much hyped and overrated television reality show—'X Factor'. People from some parts of the north of England, particularly the North East, prefix references to their relatives with the word 'our', as in 'our gran'. In the spoof at one of the character's funeral, a floral tribute in the hearse read 'R GRAN'.

[xv] Brian Forbes' classic movie *Whistle Down the Wind* was filmed around Pendle.
[xvi] Don't you dare confuse them with Blueberries. Unlike their bland American cousins, these are reet tasty!

[xvii] The title is a spoof of the song 'The Lighthouse Across the Bay' by Conrad Veidt, given regular airtime by Terry Wogan on his breakfast show in the 1970's. The imagined heights of sophistication alluded to in the poem may once again be attained, following the restoration of the hotel by Urban Splash in 2008. My experience of staying there was a little more prosaic. In the 1980s an evening meal at the Midland was most likely to come out of a tin; mandarin oranges in syrup with condensed milk offered as a dessert, served in a Pyrex bowl. Even then however, its glory was still evident beneath the peeling wallpaper and failing plumbing. The hotel contains works by the two Erics, Gill and Ravilious, and I imagine it being visited from time to time by the other one (Bartholomew).

I could not think of a more appropriate motor car in which to arrive at the Midland Hotel than an Armstrong Siddeley, but there were none in the car park when I was last there.

Morecambe Bay has always been a stopping off point for migrating birds, now immortalised in sculpture on the seafront and the focus of a new environmental tourism initiative.

Morecambe's illuminations were not a patch on Blackpool's, but during the 1950's, tableaux were lit in Happy Mount Park, which was a magnet for tourists seeking an evening stroll and perhaps a late cuppa and a Eccles cake in the park café. Meanwhile children could be ferried around the park in miniature fire engines, operated by local businessman Eric Leyland.

Lancaster, Morecambe and Heysham were locations chosen for experiments in railway electrification as early as 1904 and again in 1953 when state of the art technology meant riding around in Edwardian electric trains. The journey from Morecambe Promenade to Lancaster Green Ayre took you through Scale Hall, which represented the white heat of urban station design in 1957 when it opened (it closed for good in 1966). The station proved very popular with locals, especially due to the pram special 4d ticket which took young mums shopping in Lancaster. The station also served the nearby estates of Metroland-inspired 1920's and 30's houses. Some may well have been lived in by a man called Clive and others may well have had a Jowett Javelin parked in the Drive. These houses were also the inspiration for a series of building toys popular with both girls and boys and marketed under the trade name "Bayko", versions of which survive to this day.

East of Lancaster was the direct rail route to Skipton and Leeds, known as the Little North Western, which failed to survive the Beeching Axe; Caton being one of the sleepy halts on the route east, and Saltaire (a conceit for salt air) refers to Titus Salt's model village north of Bradford. Much of Morecambe's holiday trade came from West Yorkshire, so it is likely it was visited by people from Saltaire as well.

[XVIII] Written after a visit to Caernarfon, where the doyenne of seaside landladies still trades, terrifying us with her housekeeping. Everything smelt of embrocation and the whole place was polished to within an inch of its life. I wanted to rebel, to catch verrucas and infect my room, especially since my bathroom was down the hall, so I could have made a right mess of the hygiene! There was alas no Coal Tar soap, and the toilet paper was that soft dopey dog stuff. It should have been comb and paper 'Izal', and then I might have got a tune out of it.

[XIX] One of the most romantic and colourful attractions at the fairgrounds in Blackpool, Margate or Southport (though they all had different names) was the River Caves, where for a few shillings you were transported in a slow boat to the far corners of the globe, the waves gently lapping beneath you, and then you would emerge at the end with a very damp flourish beneath a tiny water chute! Chullo? That's Peruvian headgear don't you know.

[XX] Glen Helen is on the west coast of the Isle of Man. Pioneering aviator Amy Johnson visited and was later lost in the Thames Estuary in 1941. Her body was never recovered.

[XXI] Roman Goddess of the Grove, supplanted by St Anne.

XXII Pauline Matthews (a.k.a. the singer, Kiki Dee) hails from Sheffield. Her career has in some ways mirrored the paternoster that can be found in the Arts Tower at Sheffield University—up one minute, down the next. I caught up with her at the Bullingdon Arms, Cowley Road, Oxford (The Bully), where she performed a brief set with Carmelo Luggeri.

XXIII Gandhi visited the East End of London in 1931, residing at the Kingsley Hall in Bow. It is unlikely that he met Alice B Toklas who was the long time muse and lover of Gertrude Stein, but you never know...

XXIV This was written on the occasion of my visit to the Shard on the first weekend it opened to the public. I do not like heights but the proprietors made damn sure I could not easily throw myself off. Next time I go up I'll take a sledge hammer (unlikely). On the way up you are accompanied by a heavenly muzak choir, presumably because this is about as near to heaven as you can get in London.

XXV Male Impersonator Vesta Tilley is most frequently associated with the music hall song 'Burlington Bertie from Bow'. Celebrity photographer David Bailey's father was a taxi driver. As far as I know, there is no connection between the two.

XXVI David Bailey held a retrospective at Compressor House, Docklands in 2012. I bought a coffee in the gallery cafe after visiting the exhibition and on the receipt, at the top, it read "David Bailey's East End Thankyou"

XXVII LZ129 was the German Airship Hindenburg, destroyed by fire as it came into land at Lakehurst, New Jersey, 6th May 1937. The Zeppelin museum in Friedrichshafen contains a reconstruction of the interior of the great ship, including the salon, complete with grand piano. The Hindenburg never flew to Egypt, having been used exclusively on transatlantic services to both North and South America. However, its predecessors, including the famous Graf Zeppelin, did circumnavigate the globe. To this day there is still a degree of mystery surrounding the true cause of the Hindenburg disaster. There is no proof however that the fire was started by a stray cigarette. Egypt was a proposed port of call for the British Airships' empire run before the crash of the R101 on its maiden overseas flight, at Beauvais France, 5th October 1930. As a British Protectorate (make of that what you will) Egypt continued to be served by the Imperial Airways Company, whose flying boats called at Alexandria from 1937. Those were the days...

XXVIII Vroom and Dreesman is a major Dutch department store chain, pitching its market somewhere between Debenhams and House of Fraser. Stay OK!

is a Dutch budget hotel chain whose illuminated advertisements feature prominently on Rotterdam skyscrapers.

Holland Amerika was the major Dutch participant in the golden age of the transatlantic liners in the twenties and thirties, its flagship being the *Nieuw Amsterdam*, a name carried by four such vessels, the most famous of which was built in Rotterdam in 1937.

An 'ambtenaar' is a term usually applied to Dutch local government administrators; many Dutch people use the term pejoratively, believing that 'ambtenaren' basically "sit on their arses and do nothing, except earning wages".

XXIX Local Dutch girl Corrie Ten Boom ran the family jewellers shop in Haarlem. She provided a safe house for Jews fleeing persecution from the Nazis during the Second World War. Once on the escape route, they were hidden behind a false wall in her bedroom. A figurine placed in the shop window was the signal for safe arrival or departure. The secret room was eventually discovered and Corrie was sent to Auschwitz. Happily she survived.

XXX Completed in 1932, the dyke joining both sides of the Ijsselmeer, also known as the Zuider Zee, began a process of significant land reclamation and provided a road route between the east and west shores of this now inland sea. The dyke is 30km long and only 90m wide. Many Dutch were followers of John Calvin and he has absolutely nothing to do with the Afsluit, having died several centuries before anyone had even thought of it.

XXXI The last lines are from Sam Cooke's song 'You Send Me'.

XXXII Denkmal: The final lines come from the song 'Paper Moon' composed by Harold Arlen (lyrics by E Y Harburg and Billy Rose). The decadence and freedom of the Weimar Republic was probably best captured in Isherwood's 'I am a Camera', the inspiration for the movie musical *Cabaret* which ushered in a much darker era. Leni Riefenstahl captured the zeitgeist in her film *Triumph of the Will* in 1935. Now the gloves were well and truly off...

Kristallnacht: This represents the defining moment in the persecution of the Jews in Nazi Germany, November 1938. The name refers to the shards of broken glass that littered the streets after the pogrom. Today armed police stand guard at the site of the synagogue in Fasanenstrasse, keeping us out, and to think, all those years ago armed police were there to keep the Jews in...

Olympische Stadion Berlin: To preserve the facade of normality whilst committing unspeakable acts of persecution, torture and murder, the Nazi regime paraded the Latow brothers as an example of their 'enlightened and tolerant policy towards Jewish people', allowing them to compete in the Olympic Games of 1936. Within six weeks of the games ending, they were packed off to the camps, where they died.

Love of The Common People: Heinrich Zille was a German photographer and illustrator best known for his stereotypical caricatures of ordinary Germans in the early years of the twentieth century, thinly disguised scathing attacks on the state bureaucracy that was doing little to address the plight of the city's poorest at that time. As a result the 'Common People' took him to their hearts. Film producer Gerhardt Lamprecht made the film *Die Verufenen* based on his illustrations. A later film, entitled *Zille und Ick* (sic) revisited the same territory. Less well known was his erotic work, which found its way into the Beate Uhse Erotik Museum.

Picture of Lili: Two Marlene Dietrich films are referenced here—*Blue Angel* (1930) and *Shanghai Express* (1932). One role and song with which she is most closely associated is Lili Marlene. 'Pictures of Lily' was a hit for rock band The Who in the UK in 1967 but that was all about Lily Langtry, thus proving the necessity for keeping your Lilies in proper order.

Mies En Scène: This poem references the Lake Shore house in Chicago by Mies van der Rohe. As a disciple of the Bauhaus movement, Van de Rohe exhibited the wrong kind of Realpolitik, and as a result was forced into exile.

Japs in the Urban Jungle: 'U-boat' was the name given to many Jews who managed to remain undiscovered in Berlin throughout the war. One assumes similarly oppressed people managed to avoid the East German Secret Police (Stasi) during the Cold War era.

Shapeshifting: German architect Walter Adolph Gropius founded the Bauhaus School in 1919.

Konzert für zwei Klavierspieler: The Berliner here are the people of the city, not Kennedy's doughnuts!

XXXIII Baden Baden is a beautiful town, but new York it ain't! If you get the reference to Frank Sinatra you won't need a translation!

XXXIV The following refer to tiny fictitious but famous kingdoms—Blefescu, Grand Fenwick, Freedonia, Rubovia, Macho Grande, Brigadoon. Ron and Reg were the Kray brothers—I imagine them having a secret account in Lichtenstein, but they probably just stuffed it in the old lady's mattress.

XXXV Towards the end of the Second World War the Germans, in collusion with the Hungarian government, were anxious to erase all traces of their extermination policies. In one particularly brutal incident, hundreds of Jews were rounded up, forced to strip and shot, their bodies left to float down the river. This was immortalised in a bronze sculpture on the banks of the Danube in Budapest.

XXXVI The title of the poem is also the title of a famous film by Jean Vigo. Francine Weisweiller owned the villa Santo Sospir, where she entertained all the luminaries mentioned in this poem—Polo Picasso (daughter of Pablo), Scott and Zelda Fitzgerald, Jeanne Moreau, Coco Chanel and Lee Miller, wife of Norman Penrose and a famous war photographer in her own right. Many of the artists came to the Côte d'Azur for the light, but paradoxically tended to paint indoor scenes. Nous Deux, a famous song by Line Renaud, featured on her eponymous album in 1946. It's lovely.

XXXVII A number of Joni Mitchell's songs and albums are referenced in this poem. Look away now if you don't want to know which ones they are: 'Carey' from the album 'Blue'; The album 'Court and Spark'; 'Big Yellow Taxi', a single release featured on the album 'Ladies of the Canyon'.

XXXVIII Many tourists flock to Café Florian in St Mark's Square—it's pretty but expensive! You decide if it is worth it.

XXXIX Major Osborne Godolphin (not to be confused with Francis D'Arcy Godolphin Osborne, 12th Duke of Leeds, Envoy Extraordinary and Minister Plenipotentiary to the Holy See, 1936-1947) occupies the nearest grave to the East of John Keats' in Rome. My ancestral name is Osborne, and I was born in a little garret in Godolphin Road, Shepherds Bush—how's that for a link? Amongst the myriad famous people buried in the dissenters' cemetery in Rome are painter Asmus Carstens, and poet and contemporary of Allen Ginsberg, Gregory Corso.

XL This was the story of a balmy night time crossing from Syracuse to Valetta on an old tramp steamer in 1968.

XLI It has been quite extensively built over now, but I remember Xlendi Bay as a tiny and peaceful resort on the island of Gozo, where many Maltese from the "mainland" would take their holidays.

XLII Like Mr Gaudi's cathedral in Barcelona, this poem has, for many years, also been work in progress. This is just a small snapshot of the daily goings on, on the century old building site that is his masterpiece.

XLIII On your next trip to the Algarve (assuming you make one), you may spot a post card for sale showing a colourful character riding a donkey and smoking a pipe. This is Jorge. We sat and had a beer with Jorge and he told us all about it!

[XLIV] That's what it said on the sign!

[XLV] With apologies to anyone who suffers from the latter—I know it is not pleasant and with further apologies to anyone who had the misfortune to endure Wilson, Keppel and Betty, one of the funniest cod Egyptian vaudeville acts that ever graced a stage, if grace is the right word.

[XLVI] In 1786, a dirt poor Scottish farmer booked his passage to Jamaica. On arrival he would become one of 10,000 bonded labourers whose role was to oversee 300,000 black African slaves. Nearly all the Scots who went to Jamaica at that time were men, which goes some way to explaining why today there are more Campbells in Jamaica than there are in Scotland! The farmer's name was Robert Burns. As we now know, he did not go and as a result Scotland has this rich legacy of wonderful poetry in the Scottish dialect. But what if he had gone? Perhaps, a few years into his time there, his poetry might have sounded something like the poem you will read here.

It is no wonder there is such a rich cultural heritage emanating from Jamaica, in its music and verse forms, exported all over the world, and constantly evolving. American poet Gil Scott-Heron was descended from Jamaican Scots. When I first performed Peely Wally, my friend John called it a "real spitter". So, let's mash it up with the Gaelic massive; we wish you a rantin' readin'!

Home Thoughts from a Broad